Science Questions

What Are Clouds Made Of?

by Rebecca Pettiford

Bullfrog Books

Ideas for Parents and Teachers

Bullfrog Books let children practice reading informational text at the earliest reading levels. Repetition, familiar words, and photo labels support early readers.

Before Reading

- Discuss the cover photo. What does it tell them?

- Look at the picture glossary together. Read and discuss the words.

Read the Book

- "Walk" through the book and look at the photos. Let the child ask questions. Point out the photo labels.

- Read the book to the child, or have him or her read independently.

After Reading

- Prompt the child to think more. Ask: Clouds are made of water. Did you know about the water cycle before reading this book? What more would you like to learn?

Bullfrog Books are published by Jump!
5357 Penn Avenue South
Minneapolis, MN 55419
www.jumplibrary.com

Library of Congress Cataloging-in-Publication Data

Names: Pettiford, Rebecca, author.
Title: What are clouds made of? / by Rebecca Pettiford.
Description: Minneapolis, MN: Jump!, Inc., [2023]
Series: Science questions | Includes index.
Audience: Ages 5–8
Identifiers: LCCN 2022011507 (print)
LCCN 2022011508 (ebook)
ISBN 9798885240536 (hardcover)
ISBN 9798885240543 (paperback)
ISBN 9798885240550 (ebook)
Subjects: LCSH: Clouds—Juvenile literature.
Classification: LCC QC921.35 .P49 2023 (print)
LCC QC921.35 (ebook)
DDC 551.57/6—dc23/eng20220517
LC record available at
https://lccn.loc.gov/2022011507
LC ebook record available at
https://lccn.loc.gov/2022011508

Editor: Jenna Gleisner
Designer: Emma Bersie

Photo Credits: Nataliia K/Shutterstock, cover; Yaisomanang/Shutterstock, 1; media-ja/Shutterstock, 3; VisanuPhotoshop/Shutterstock, 4; Zdravinjo/Dreamstime, 5; ValerioMei/Shutterstock, 6–7; Donald34/iStock, 8–9, 23br; somchaii/Shutterstock, 10–11; ITSUKY/Shutterstock, 12–13, 23tr; cdstocks/Shutterstock, 14, 23bl; Lukas Jonaitis/Alamy, 15; John Sirlin/Alamy, 16–17; PBXStudio/Shutterstock, 18; StudioDin/Shutterstock, 19; narikan/Shutterstock, 20–21; Nelli Covali/Dreamstime, 23tl; Zurbagan/Shutterstock, 24.

Printed in the United States of America at Corporate Graphics in North Mankato, Minnesota.

Table of Contents

Floating Water

Max looks up at the sky.

He sees clouds.

What are they made of?

Water!

lake

Water is in oceans.

It is in rivers and lakes, too.

The Sun heats water.

It turns into water vapor.

We cannot see it.

It rises.

water vapor

High in the sky, it cools.
It turns into small drops
of water.

Dust floats in the air.

The drops stick to the dust.

Together, they form clouds.

Some drops freeze in the clouds.

They turn into ice.

They fall as hail.

hail

Others turn into snow.
They fall as snowflakes.

snowflake

Look!

The sky has dark clouds.

They hold a lot of water.

The clouds get too heavy.
Drops of rain fall from them.

raindrops

Time to play!

The Water Cycle

Clouds form from water and dust. This is part of the water cycle. Take a look!

2. High in the air, it cools. It turns into drops of water, ice, or snow.

3. It falls from clouds as rain, hail, or snowflakes.

1. The Sun heats water in rivers, lakes, and oceans. It turns into water vapor. It rises.

4. It falls into rivers, lakes, and oceans. The cycle starts over.

Picture Glossary

dust
Tiny particles of something like dirt that gather on surfaces or float in the air.

floats
Rests or moves in the air.

freeze
To become solid or turn into ice at a very low temperature.

water vapor
A gas made of drops of water mixed with air.

Index

To Learn More

Finding more information is as easy as 1, 2, 3.

❶ Go to www.factsurfer.com

❷ Enter "whatarecloudsmadeof" into the search box.

❸ Choose your book to see a list of websites.